DOMINICA'S STORY

A Life of Courage, Hope, and Love

s

By

DOMINICA ANNESE

As told to Kate Loftus-Graney & Kaitlin McQuade
Foreword and Epilogue by Francine Annese Apy

DOMINICA'S STORY

A Life of Courage, Hope, and Love

Publisher: SoulFilling, LLC

CONTENTS

Foreword

By the grace of God, Dominica made it to the USA, which became her home.

My name is Francine Annese Apy and I am Dominica's youngest of four daughters. Everyone we have ever met during our lives has been fascinated by our mother's story. For as long as I can remember we wanted to write and publish my mother's story, as inspiration for those who overcame a difficult childhood or enjoy reading stories of survival and the power of having the right mindset, under any circumstances.

While Dominica overcame so much in her life, marrying my father and being a mother to us was her greatest achievement and brought her tremendous joy. Even thougshe was separated from her mother at five years of age, her natural instincts and common sense allowed her to thrive in a matriarchal role. There is nothing she is prouder of than my sisters and me. She loved raising, nurturing, and guiding us to be bright, kind, independent, educated, and confident women.

We pray that this book will serve others inspiration, hope, and faith, as well as a reminder of the power of a positive mindset. My mother emulated these characteristics and believed that is what allowed her to flourish and become the person she is today. She wants the same for everyone she meets, and especially for the people of Ukraine.

Many thanks to Kate Graney Loftus and Kaitlyn

McQuaid for bringing this story to life. Our family will be forever grateful to you both.

Introduction

Dominica Myskiw Annese has stunning clear and beautiful blue eyes and silver blonde hair. Her warm embrace upon meeting for the first time is equally striking. She radiates love, care, and empathy. For these reasons alone Dominica is a remarkable woman, but when you learn about the incredible, nearly unbelievable story of her early life, you realize the true depths of Dominica's inner strength and resilience, which today manifest themselves so clearly through her devotion to her family, particularly her 11 grandchildren and four great grandchildren.

The word "Ukraine" actually means "borderland." And indeed, the country we today know as Ukraine has had the dubious honor of historically being a border between larger, often imperialistic states—Poland-Lithuania in the 16th and 17th centuries, Austria-Hungary and Russia in the 18th and 19th centuries, and Germany and the Soviet Union in the 20th century. While the Ukrainian language shares many traits with its fellow Slavic languages such as Russian and Polish, it is a distinct and rich language with a unique alphabet and its own singular expressions and words. Ukrainians also have their own cultural traditions—beautiful, embroidered clothing, folk tales, and food. Another unique thing about Ukrainians is that many of them chose to remain part of the Roman Catholic Church when the Russian Orthodox and Greek Orthodox Churches broke with Rome and the Pope back in 1595. The Ukrainian Greek Catholic Church remains a powerful force both in Ukraine and among Ukrainians living in the United States and elsewhere in the world.

Before 2022, Ukraine was a young, but hopeful country, updated with the war) having gained its independence when the Soviet Union collapsed in 1991. The Ukrainian people have twice shown the world their democratic and freedom loving spirit since gaining independence—in 2004's "Orange Revolution" when they rejected unfair and rigged election results and demanded free and fair elections, and in 2014's "EuroMaidan" movement when they refused to let then President Victor Yanukovich turn Ukraine away from the people's chosen path towards integration with Europe and the rest of the democratic world. While the eastern part of Ukraine remains disputed and under threat from Russian occupation, the country and its young people in particular, are determined that Ukraine will persevere and become a modern, prosperous, independent and democratic state in Europe. It seems today's young Ukrainians have the same inner strength and will to survive and make a better life for themselves and their families that also characterize Dominica Myskiw Annese.

At the end of World War One (1918), many Ukrainians hoped that they would finally be given their own state, after being part of others' empires for so long. Instead, the territory of today's Ukraine was divided between the newly created Polish state and the communist led Soviet Union, which had replaced the Russian Empire. The small city of Staryi Sambir, located to the southwest of the larger city of Lviv, had a substantial Ukrainian population, as well as many Poles and Jewish citizens. After 1918, Staryi Sambir became part of the new Polish state, and while Ukrainians shared a Catholic faith with their new Polish leaders, Ukrainians were generally not allowed to learn at school in their own language, instead receiving their instruction in Polish. In September 1939, a mere twenty years after achieving a fragile independence, Poland was once again divided between two greater powers—Germany under the Nazi leadership of Adolf Hitler, and Soviet Russia under the leadership of Josef Stalin. In September 1939 Sambir was briefly occupied by the German army before it retreated in the face of the Soviet Russian Red Army, which occupied the city.

The Myskiw Family

One of the Ukrainian families trying to make sense of the bewildering political changes washing over the Staryi Sambir region was that of Raymond (Roman) and Katherine (Katarina) Myskiw. Raymond Myskiw was a successful farmer, owning horses, cows and a substantial amount of property. Raymond was successful enough to employ several people to help with the farm work, while Katherine Myskiw took care of the couple's five young daughters—Mary, the oldest, then Ann, Sonya, Olga, and the baby, Dominica, who was born on January 12, 1938. (Dominica's papers suggest that the Myskiw property might have been closer to the villages of Isaji and Turka, which were located a bit to the south of Sambir, closer to the start of the Dniester River. See Map One) This part of Polish Ukraine was populated mostly by farmers in the 1930s and 1940s, and while conditions were somewhat primitive—for example, there was no running water or electricity by comparison with Ukrainians living across the border in Soviet Russia, Ukrainians in Poland were lucky. (In the early 1930s the Ukrainian people in Soviet Russia suffered horribly from Stalin's collective farming reforms, which led to a terrible famine in Ukraine, the *Holodomor*.) When the Soviet Red Army occupied Polish Ukraine in 1939, life was not easy; though the Russians were somewhat more willing to let Ukrainians speak and read in their own language than the Poles had been, they repressed all forms of religious practice, including Catholicism.

Map One: *South-Eastern Poland in the 1930s (The cities of Sambir and Turka are right above the "P" in the Carpathian Mountain label.)*

In June of 1941, Adolf Hitler carried the campaign of war and terror that Germany had already inflicted on France, Belgium, Britain, and some parts of Poland into the Russian-controlled areas of Poland, including Sambir. German troops arrived in the Lviv-Staryi Sambir region in July 1941, and the region remained under German occupation until the Soviet Red Army fought its way back and "liberated" the town in August 1944. The Ukrainian, Polish, and Jewish citizens of the Staryi Sambir region all suffered terrible hardships during this horrific period of war. Even among the hundreds of thousands of stories of loss and terror during World War Two, Dominica Myskiw's

experience stands out. (See Map Two)

Map Two: *Soviet advances against Germans from 1
August 1943 to 31 December 1944: to 1 December 1943 to
30 April 1944 to 19 August 1944 to 31 December 1944.
Sambir / Lviv region fighting Summer 1944.*

The Second World War Comes to Staryi Sambir

When you ask Dominica Myskiw Annese about her experiences during the Second World War, her beautiful face crumples into a portrait of sadness. "It was total chaos," she says, her eyes filling with tears. "It was like 9/11. You have no idea. The noise, the smoke, everyone crying." During the summer of 1944, Dominica, who was then only about 4 or 5 years old, and her older sister Sonya, who was then about 12 or 13 years old, were caught in the horror and violence that the fighting between the German Nazis and Soviet Russians brought. Both girls were hit by shrapnel and bullets, with Dominica receiving serious wounds to her leg and back, which left lasting and distinctive scars. Dominica recalls how painful her wounds were, and that there was no anesthetic when the doctors removed the shrapnel from her, "only a rag stuffed in my mouth". Characteristically optimistic, however, she notes that, "If they hadn't removed them though, I wouldn't be able to walk today, would I?"

Desperate to save his daughters in the midst of the danger and confusion, Raymond Myskiw gently loaded the wounded girls into a horse-drawn wagon and took them to the nearest hospital in Sambir. Dominica remembers her time in the hospital as nightmarish. "In the hospital, people were lined up like animals. We were lying next to German soldiers. We were hungry. I remember being given an apple and being so hungry, but only eating half and putting the other half in my pocket to share with my sister." The continued fighting made it impossible for Dominica and Sonya's parents to visit them in the hospital—the girls didn't know if the rest of their family was dead or alive, but they feared the worst.

How overwhelming and terrifying this experience must have been for Dominica and Sonya. It is hard to believe, then, that the war was not done with them yet. One of Adolf Hitler's plans for Germany, a main motivation for starting World War Two, was to create a "Greater Germany" that would provide more "living room" (*lebensraum*) for the German people. Part of this effort by the Nazis to conquer non-German areas was to take "suitable" children back to Germany to be raised by German families and to become citizens of the new German Empire. The Nazis placed a lot of emphasis on physical appearance and believed that children who shared the blond hair and blue eyes that supposedly characterized "pure Germans" were the most valuable. As little Dominica Myskiw had exquisite blue eyes and long blond hair, she was highly desired by the German government as a potential future German citizen. German soldiers tried to seize Dominica to take her to Germany, leaving behind her older sister Sonya, who had dark hair and dark eyes. Sonya showed incredible bravery in stopping the German soldiers, saying, "If you take her, you must take me too!" Sonya would not leave her younger sister alone. So, the girls again became victims of the war, this time being forced onto freight trains headed back to Germany, along with grievously wounded German soldiers.

Dominica still marvels at the strength of her older sister at that moment so many years ago. "She was just a little girl too," Dominica remembers. "And there was no one to take care of her, but she was determined to take care of me." It was only the first of many times that Sonya would stand up for her younger sister as their frightening wartime journey continued.

A Train to Germany

Remembering the train trip away from her family and to Germany is, understandably, very difficult for Dominica. The Germans shaved her beautiful long hair before the trip to protect against lice, and there was very, very little water or food. She remembers how grateful she was when at one point the train stopped and someone offered her a ladle of water. Nothing ever tasted as good or seemed as precious as that water, she remembers. The young sisters traveled for days, further and further from their home, through Poland, Czechoslovakia, and Hungary and finally arriving in Germany. Dominica and Sonya were first placed in a camp for "Displaced Persons" (of which there were, sadly, many), and then, some months later, after the German surrender in May 1945, were sent to a new children's center in the German city of Prien, in the state of Bavaria (located about 30 miles southeast of the city of Munich). (Prien is also sometimes known as "Prien am Chiemsee".)

Dominica and Sonya would spend 3 long years in the "International Displaced Children's Center at Kloster Indersdorf" in Prien. The Children's Center was a network of hostels and schools located in several buildings in Prien, including a hotel and autobahn rest stop where Hitler once stayed, and the buildings of a former Catholic convent. The Children's center was run in part by the new United Nations Relief and Rehabilitation Agency (UNRRA), with the help of the U.S. Army and some local Catholic nuns. It opened in November 1945 and it is estimated that over 1,000 children spent time there in the post-war years. The children were from more than 20 countries from all over Europe. Some, like Dominica and Sonya, had been forcibly taken from their homes in Eastern Europe by the Germans. Others had been orphaned by the Holocaust and had just been liberated from the concentration camp at nearby Dachau. All were traumatized, a fact not lost on the UNRRA personnel who helped to run the Children's Center. Greta Fischer, a social worker at the Center in the post-war period, notes that the staff there understood how fragile the children there were, and that they "tried to do the right thing" for them."[1]

Dominica's spirit is strong enough to recollect some of the good aspects of living at the Children's Center. For one, she and her sister Sonya at least were together. The girls lived with 25-30 other children in a large room. Each child had a cot and one box for their personal belongings, which they stored under their cot. Dominica remembers treasuring a doll made out of a sock with button eyes, and how an older boy made a swing for her in a tree on the cloister grounds, because she loved to swing. Dominica remembers that she would "swing on it every day, for as long as I could." She also remembers getting a "Red Cross Box" that contained a pencil, an eraser, and a yo-yo, and believing it was "the greatest treasure." She once made a piece of gum that a soldier gave her last an entire week! Remembering these small kindnesses prompts Dominica to urge her children and grandchildren to

---

[1] Kloster Indersdorf 1945-48", http://kloster-indersdorf-1945-48.blogspot.com/p/post-war-childrens-centers-at-kloster.html.

"appreciate the life you have"—the years of deprivation and loss in Prien certainly taught her to appreciate the simple gift of being alive.

Photo One: *Dominica Myskiw at the Kloster Indersdorf Children's Center in late 1945 or early 1946. Dominica is the beautiful child in the back row holding the teacher's hand.*

The administrators of the Children's Center did try to help the children keep ties with their native languages and cultures. Dominica remembers very vividly a woman at the center who taught Ukrainian folk dances to the children, and who made for Dominica the beautiful embroidered Ukrainian blouse that is today probably her most cherished possession. (She made sure that each of her four daughters wore it and were photographed in it before having it carefully preserved. See Photo One) Dominica also sang in a Ukrainian choir at the Children's Center. There were also opportunities to interact with local German children, and in fact Dominica became fluent in German during her years in Prien! She particularly remembers her close friend Ingrid, a German girl, and once being photographed at the orphanage wearing Ingrid's dress. In fact, Ingrid's family loved Dominica so much that they wanted to adopt her, but of course, Dominica and Sonya did not want to be separated, and, fearing and believing that their family in Ukraine was dead, Sonya began to make plans for the two sisters to begin a new life in America.

In order to leave Germany and immigrate to America, the girls needed a sponsor and a guarantee of a job. Sonya was able to get secure permission for herself to travel to the U.S., but again, she would not leave Dominica and insisted that her younger sister be allowed to travel with her to begin a new life in America. But Dominica was still so undernourished and frail after years of war and life in the orphanage, that the authorities would not let Dominica travel with Sonya – they were afraid that she would not survive the long journey! So, for another long year, Sonya tried to earn extra money in Germany to pay for extra food for Dominica and for their future passage to America, mostly by selling door to door the clothes donated to the war "orphan" children by the Salvation Army and Red Cross. Dominica remembers her sister urging her to "Eat, eat more!" so that the authorities would let her join Sonya on the trip to America. Finally, in the fall of 1948 Dominica was declared healthy enough to travel, and the next phase of her amazing journey began.

Coming to America

D ominica and her sister Sonya traveled to America in the fall of 1948 on a re-commissioned U.S. Army troopship called the *USAT General W.M. Black*, arriving in New York Harbor on October 30. The ship sailed directly in front of the Statue of Liberty and NYFD ships greeted the new arrivals with celebratory spouts of water! (See Photo Two).

Photo Two*: The USAT General W.M. Black arriving in New York Harbor in October 1938.*

When she first arrived in America, Dominica lived with two different foster families for several years, one in New York City and one in Johnson City, New York. Her older sister eventually married and settled near Syracuse, New York and as soon as she was able, called for Dominica to come live with her and her young family. Dominica remembers how important her teachers were to her during these first years in America—besides her sister, no one had a bigger impact on her than her teachers. They "made our lives," she says. Dominica especially remembers a very kind teacher named Mrs. Gibson, who would make her feel so special and "not so alone." Dominica quickly learned to speak English, in part by spending every summer in summer school, and so added English to her native Ukrainian and the German she had learned at the Children's Center. She was now trilingual!

Dominica also worked "at any job she could find," at a children's store, as a receptionist at a photo studio, and at the Ben Franklin 5 and 10 store, to earn a little spending money. She remembers only buying the best quality clothes in neutral colors, "so that they would last the longest." She didn't have a lot of things, but they would be of good quality. All her hard academic and other work paid off, and she graduated from high school in 1958, just a few years after arriving in the US. Dominica stresses how important she believes education to be, and how, even though she never had the chance to go to college, she would "force herself to read" to keep learning and knowing more and more.

Many Ukrainians who had arrived in the United States after the Second World War were able to re-establish contact with their families in Ukraine, which was now entirely a part of the Soviet Union. (Although the Soviet Russian authorities liked to pretend to the world that Ukraine was a "sovereign" country, and even got the "Ukrainian Soviet Socialist Republic" a seat at the United Nations, in reality, the country was closely controlled by the communist government in Moscow.) Many other Ukrainian survivors of World War Two in America were like Dominica, not knowing if their families were still alive or not, or whether they remembered them or not. Dominica remembers the pain of not knowing her parents during these years, or even knowing if they were alive. She says that especially when she was in Germany, she remembers missing her mother so much, and wondering what her mother looked like.

An Amazing Discovery

The close-knit community of Ukrainians in America had started Ukrainian-language newspapers, and these newspapers served as a means of communication between Ukrainians in the Soviet Union and Ukrainians in America. (The Cold War tensions between the U.S. and the Soviet Union in the 1950s made communication and travel very difficult, but some information did get through, especially in these newspapers.) Families living in Soviet Ukraine who had lost children in the Second World War would sometimes place advertisements in these Ukrainian-American newspapers, searching for any information about their missing loved ones. In the early 1950s, through this amazing communication network (remember, this is way before the internet, email or even the fax machine!), Dominica and Sonya found out some unbelievable news—their family in Ukraine had survived the war and was alive and well!

While in the German orphanage, Dominica and Sonya had been visited by a Ukrainian man named Mychajlo Myskiw who had lost his two daughters during the course of the war. By coincidence, he had the same last name as Dominica and Sonya and came from the same village. Mychajlo had heard about Dominica and her sister being in the German orphanage and believed that they could possibly be his missing daughters. Once he met them, he quickly realized that they were not. Mychajlo later moved to New Jersey but continued to communicate with the part of his family that remained in Staryi Sambir. He was thus connected with Dominica and Sonya's father, also still living in Staryi Sambir, who once mentioned his two lost daughters, one with blue eyes and blonde hair and the other with very dark eyes. Mychajlo finally made the connection between Dominica and Sonya, the two young girls who he had met years earlier, and their father, the man he knew in Staryi Sambir. Mychajlo put an advertisement out in a Ukrainian-American newspaper, Svoboda, published in Jersey City, New Jersey, that Sonya often read. The advertisement sought out the two girls in hopes of putting them in contact with their family who had been missing them for so many years. After nearly a decade of silence and agonized worry, the sisters were able to write letters to and even sometimes share telephone calls with their parents and sisters in Ukraine. It seemed nothing short of a miracle!

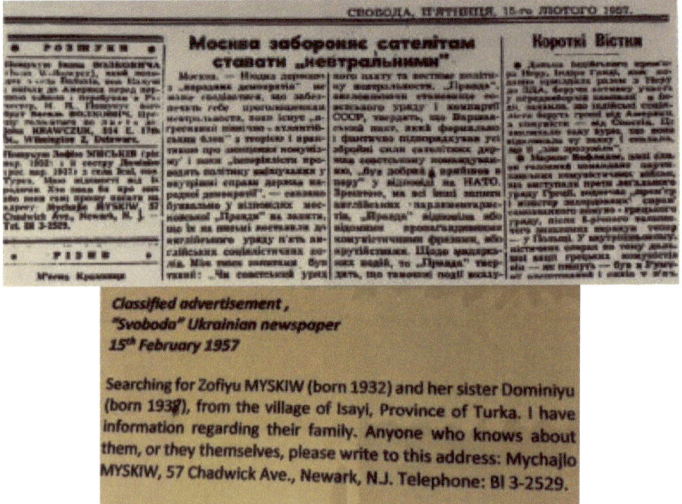

Classified advertisement,
"Svoboda" Ukrainian newspaper
15th February 1957

Searching for Zofiyu MYSKIW (born 1932) and her sister Dominiyu (born 1937), from the village of Isayi, Province of Turka. I have information regarding their family. Anyone who knows about them, or they themselves, please write to this address: Mychajlo MYSKIW, 57 Chadwick Ave., Newark, N.J. Telephone: BI 3-2529.

Photo Three: *Advertisement in Svoboda newspaper in Ukrainian and English*

Dominica's life took another wonderful turn soon after high school, when she met Frank Annese, who was then a Junior at the University of Notre Dame in Indiana. Dominica had returned from Syracuse to Johnson City to be the maid-of-honor in the wedding of one of her best friends from her time living there. At the wedding she met the handsome and charming Frank, who told her that she "looked like a beauty queen" (she did!). She and Frank were married in 1962, and Dominica remembers how wonderful it was to be welcomed into Frank's large Italian family. Frank, whom Dominica describes as "being able to sell ice to Eskimos," began his long and remarkably successful career by working at Mohawk Data Sciences in Herkimer, New York. The young couple had four daughters in rapid succession—Michelle, Yvonne, Andrea and Francine.

Following Frank's success as a salesman, Redbook Magazine ran a story following several young couples who recently came into wealth, including Frank and Dominica Annese. The article picked up shortly after the family had moved from Concord, Massachusetts to Syracuse, New York into a four-bedroom colonial house that Dominica decorated and furnished herself. Thanks to Frank's hard work they could now afford fur coats, Cadillac cars, and vacations to the Virgin Islands. However, the greatest reward for Dominica was her newfound ability to connect with her parents. She stated that, "To me, that has been the biggest thing about having all this money. If we hadn't had it, I guess I would never see my parents again." No matter what changed in her life, family always remained vitally important to Dominica.

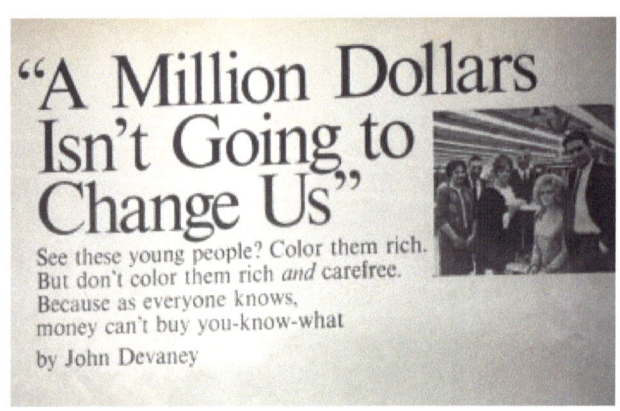

Photo Four: *Redbook Magazine article*

While the thought of having four daughters under the age of five might seem a bit daunting, Dominica remembers the years in Herkimer with her "four little dolls" as "the happiest years of my life." "Oh, how I adored them," she says of her daughters. Dominica recalls how in the early days in Herkimer, she did not have a car, so she would pull all the girls in a toboggan to the grocery store in winter or tow them on a bicycle in the summer! She always dressed the four girls in matching outfits and loved being the mother to them that she had not had the chance to have in her own life. Not everything was easy; it was difficult for Dominica when friends would talk about their parents' high-status jobs and then ask her about her parents, or ask Dominica where she had gone to school, after snootily mentioning their own high-priced college educations. But Dominica resolved that "no one was going to make me feel bad for who I was," and tried to be grateful for "what I did have, in my heart and brain," and of course her growing and beautiful family, instead of focusing on the deprivations of her past.

A Miraculous Reunion

When Dominica was pregnant with her daughter Francine in 1968, her husband Frank gave her what she calls "the most wonderful gift that anyone could have ever given me." After some ultimately unsuccessful attempts to find a way to travel to the Soviet Ukraine, a very difficult endeavor at the height of the Cold War, Dominica began to despair that she would never actually see again the family that she knew was still alive "behind the Iron Curtain." During a brief thaw in the Cold War, however, the Soviet Union agreed to allow a small number of elderly and ill Soviet citizens to take "good will" trips to the United States to be reunited with family. Amazingly, Raymond and Katherine Myskiw were granted the precious visas necessary for such a visit, and in 1968 they made the trip from Soviet Ukraine to New York, where Frank and Dominica's sister Sonya picked them up and brought them to Boston, where the Annese family was then living. Raymond was gravely ill, having recently had a stroke, and was carried off the plane in a stretcher. But they were in America, and soon, Dominica was reunited with them. Dominica remembers that upon seeing her for the first time in almost 25 years, her mother asked Dominica to unzip her dress and show her the scars from the war, to confirm the long hoped for truth—that this was her daughter. It was, and the reunited family enjoyed nearly six precious months together in America.

All these years later, Dominica still marvels at the unlikelihood of her parents' journey to America. "They came from a village that had only one car," she says. "They had never been in a car and were used to walking miles and miles to get anywhere. And suddenly here they are, getting on a plane and flying across the world to meet two girls who may or may not be their daughters. Can you imagine?"

Map 5
The Oblasts and Raions of former Eastern Galicia and Bukovina in the Ukrainian SSR, 1972

Map Three: Soviet Ukraine in the 1970s, at the time of the Myskiw's visit to America.

Dominica has wonderful memories of this precious period of reunion with her parents. "I became so close to them," she remembers. "Especially my father. I had really not thought of him too much over the years—I had missed my mother so much. But he was wonderful, and we became so close." Her father's health was not good—in addition to recovering from his stroke, he had extensive dental work done in the U.S., and sometimes "could only eat oatmeal, though he would eat bigger and bigger bowls every day!" Her father was amazed by the level of technological innovation that existed in America in the 1970s—dishwashers, vacuum cleaners, telephones, televisions, cars, and planes! He also marveled at his daughter's mastery of these different gadgets. Dominica remembers her father asking her all the time, "How did you learn how to use all these things? How did you ever learn to speak English?" Sometimes, her father would get very pensive, and even cry "big tears," Dominica says. She would tease him and say, "Father, why are you crying again?" But he would look at her with love and amazement (and tears), and say, "Dominiya, we looked and looked for you everywhere, and no one knew where you were. And here you are." It must have seemed truly miraculous to Raymond Myskiw (and who is to say it wasn't?!).

Dominica's mother, Katherine, was "a little bundle of energy," Dominica remembers. "She was always jumping around and talking and laughing." Katherine Myskiw especially took a shining to her son-in-law Frank (she "adored him") and would "talk and talk and talk" to Frank, despite the fact that she could not speak a word of English and Frank could not speak any Ukrainian. Eventually, Dominica taught Frank how to say "Yes, mother," in Ukrainian ("*Tak, tak, mama*"), and he would sit for hours and listen to her and just keep nodding and saying "*Tak, tak, mama*". Despite the better medical care in the United States, Raymond's health continued to deteriorate, and he began to think about going back to Staryi Sambir in Ukraine, his lifelong home. Raymond knew he was nearing the end of his life, and, as wrenching as it was to leave the daughters he had already lost for so long, he wanted to spend his last days at home in Ukraine. So sadly, Raymond and Katherine made plans to return home, in possession of precious new memories and, in Raymond's case, one of Frank's suits! Raymond had never owned a suit, and he cried when Frank gave it to him, explaining that "I have wanted a suit like this my whole life." When Raymond did pass on a few months later in Ukraine, he was buried in Frank's suit, his casket carried through the village on the way to the church as a sign of respect.

A Grateful Heart

Dominica's life after her parents returned to Ukraine resumed its busy, happy rhythm. Frank's business grew, her "four little dolls" grew, and Dominica gave thanks every day for all the blessings of her life. "I always tried to be grateful," she remembers. "Every day I would think about and write about who I wanted to be, about my goals, about how to be a good person, about what I loved about people." As her family prospered, and beautiful things, experiences and trips became more regular, Dominica enjoyed and appreciated it all, but always kept in her mind that "while money can buy you things, it can't make you happy." For her happiness, she had her family, both in Ukraine and here in America, and her faith that "everything that happens in our lives is supposed to happen." More happiness came in 1990, when the Soviet Union fell and Dominica and Sonya were able to return to Staryi Sambir to visit their family there, with Dominica bringing her daughter Francine, and Sonya bringing Stephanie, one of her five children (all of whom speak Ukrainian) as well.

Dominica's sisters in Ukraine had also made full lives for themselves despite the hardships of the Soviet era. Her oldest sister, Mary, had one son who was born blind, but nonetheless became a respected professor of history at one of Ukraine's leading universities. This son in turn had two children, one of whom came to visit Dominica and Frank when she was a teenager, and "was so, so talented and bright. She could play the piano and the violin just beautifully, and walked around with an encyclopedia, so eager to learn English," Dominica remembers. Her sister Olga had many children—either 8 or 9—one of whom emigrated to Italy and started her own business. Dominica and Frank once had the chance to visit this niece and her family in Italy, and Dominica remembers the comical scene: "I was translating my niece's Ukrainian into English, other people were speaking Italian, and at one point I turned to Frank and just started talking to him in Ukrainian, and he looked at me so strangely!" While Dominica had once felt so lonely because she had so little family when everyone else seemed to have so much, eventually she was able to meet and spend time with many of her aunts, nieces, and nephews. She and Frank were also able to visit Ukraine in the mid-2000s and to attend her niece's wedding. Today, her own daughters are in touch with their Ukrainian (and Italian!) cousins through Facebook, and she hopes that her grandchildren will carry on the relationships and traditions.

Dominica and her husband Frank have enjoyed their lives to the fullest and spent much time in recent years traveling the world. The two of them set sail on cruises through the Adriatic Sea, the Mediterranean Sea, and along rivers spanning from Prague to Budapest. They also traveled to Italy to visit the village where Frank's grandparents came from. Dominica notes that she would love to return to Italy in the future to see the country and visit some family.

After moving to Florida nearly 20 years ago, Dominica found community in a group of women with Ukrainian heritage. Together, they wear beautiful

Ukrainian blouses, raise money to send to Ukraine and cook delicious Ukrainian foods. Among Dominica's favorite Ukrainian dishes to cook is *holubtsi*, a stuffed cabbage dish like pigs in a blanket. She will make a whole crockpot of them to share on occasion. Finding a community of people with Ukrainian heritage has allowed Dominica to feel "reborn" by sharing her past and culture openly with others.

Dominica and Frank have remained involved with Frank's alma mater, Notre Dame, throughout the years. The two of them show their support by traveling to South Bend and other locations around the country on occasion to cheer for the university's football team. They are also the generous benefactors of the Dominica and Frank Annese Fellowships for Graduate Study at the Nanovic Institute for European Studies at the University of Notre Dame, where Dominica also serves as a member of the Institute's Governing Board. Through their philanthropy, dozens of young students, many from Ukraine, and others from different parts of Eastern Europe, have been able to study at this world-famous institution. The interdisciplinary fellowship supports students as they write about European issues in many different disciplines, contributing to an important field of research. Many focus on the importance of culture and language to various countries, something that is especially relevant to Ukraine. After meeting several of the students from Ukraine in previous years, Dominica was surprised to discover that many of them spoke primarily Russian. She learned that they had been taught Russian, not Ukrainian, in their schools. Despite the hardships that these young people and so many others in Ukraine have faced, Dominica knows that Ukrainians will never give up.

On February 24th, 2022, Russia invaded Ukraine. The war has devastated the country and started the largest refugee crisis in Europe since World War II. This has caused heartbreak around the world and especially for those of Ukrainian heritage. Ukraine has seen years of political turmoil. Pro-Russian separatists have been waging war in the Donbas region since 2014. Tensions increased over the years with the 2014 Russian invasion of Crimea and the Maidan Revolution following the Ukrainian government's decision not to pursue an agreement with the EU. For years, those in Ukraine have been concerned about Russia's encroachment on their territory and how it might end. In 2022, those fears came to pass. Putin made the decision to invade Ukraine citing a fraudulent desire to "demilitarization" and "denazification", all while denying the existence of Ukrainian statehood separate from Russia. Tens of thousands have died and millions have been displaced. Dominica notes that what is happening now is similar to what she experienced during World War II. "It's like nothing has changed," Dominica remarked.

With the invasion of Ukraine came newfound international attention towards the country. In the past, Dominica recalls people not even knowing what Ukraine was. She recalls a moment when after filling out paperwork for a driver's license, the clerk asked her where in the United States Ukraine was located. The clerk did not even know Ukraine was a country! Dominica's heritage has always been important to her, but she never expected Ukraine to be at the forefront of so many people's minds.

During the COVID-19 pandemic, Dominica spent her time in both Saratoga Springs, New York, and Naples, Florida. During this period, her sister Sonya passed away. This loss proved to be very difficult for her family since because of COVID restrictions, they were limited in the amount of contact they could have with her and one another during her passing. Sonya had a traditional Ukrainian Greek Catholic funeral in Syracuse, New York. It was held outside due to COVID restrictions, and was attended by Sonya's five children and many others.

Throughout her life, Dominica's sister Sonya had remained deeply connected to her Ukrainian roots. She arrived in this country at the age of 18, having already spent her formative years in Ukraine and other parts of Europe. Once in the U.S., Sonya married a Ukrainian man and remained involved with the greater Ukrainian community. Sonya's children speak Ukrainian and were raised with Ukrainian culture ingrained in their everyday life. Sonya always remained deeply devoted to Dominica. Sonya spent years protecting Dominica as her guardian, during the long years in Germany, and continued to be heavily involved in her life once the two sisters came to the United States. The two of them even lived next door to each other in Syracuse at one point in their lives before Dominica moved to Boston. Sonya also shared with Dominica and her family fruits and vegetables from her bountiful garden that she loved to tend to. The two of them would care for their gardens together, sharing their passions with each other. From

Ukraine to Germany, to the United States, Dominica and Sonya retained a deep connection that can never be broken.

Photo Five: *Dominica and Sonya as children wearing traditional Ukrainian blouses.*

Over the past couple of years, Dominica's family has grown and celebrated important milestones and moments. Most recently on September 8, 2022, she and Frank celebrated 60 years of marriage. Her family also has welcomed four great-grandchildren! Dominica has attended with pride many of her grandchildren's college and high school graduations. Three of her granddaughters have recently married in ceremonies she attended. Dominica has many hopes for her grandchildren and great-grandchildren. She hopes that they learn to never take anything for granted because, as she learned early in her life, it can be taken away in an instant. Dominica notes that it is up to them and their generation to decide the future of the United States. They will have to discern what is right or wrong for them and for others. And most importantly, she says that they will get out there and vote!

While Dominica's early life was full of war, suffering, and loneliness, she says that overall "there have been so many more blessings than bad things," and she hopes so much that her children, grandchildren, and great-grandchildren also appreciate the lives they have been given in the same way that she has grown to appreciate hers. While Dominica says that she has "learned when to hide" her past, and to "always be smiling and laughing," in her later years her Ukrainian heritage and the amazing story of her early life have become more important to her.

The hardships of her early life have made the incredible joys of her current life—family most of all— even more meaningful for Dominica Myskiw Annese, and the one thing she wishes the most for her children and grandchildren is that "they appreciate every single day and every single thing." It is clear that this remarkable woman sure has, and for that, she is an inspiration.

Epilogue

So, there it is. My mom's story of surviving an unimaginably difficult childhood torn apart by war and navigating through adulthood. Dominica's tale is one of resilience, joy, and unwavering optimism, all wrapped around her unshakable faith, belief in herself, and her ability to articulate her personal narrative. She authored the chapters of her life as best she could and always sought people she could learn from and grow and evolve with. Her determination is clear: she refuses to let her challenging past hinder her from living her best and most fulfilling life, even still at the time of this writing, in her 86th year.

We may not have control over many aspects of our journey through life, but one thing my mother firmly believes is that we can control our mindset to help drive positive outcomes. Despite her darkest days growing up and even now, she remains resolute that we all have the choice every day to wake up and seek joy, optimism, hope, and goodness, or that we can choose the opposite. It's evident which path Dominica has chosen which allowed her to lead a life filled with abundance and a heart free of bitterness and regret.

In the summer of 2023, an opportunity arose for my mother to give back to her Ukrainian heritage in a full-circle manner. A local nonprofit organization, dedicated to assisting families' transitions into our community, approached her. They were working with a Ukrainian family who had recently relocated to Saratoga Springs, NY, and they needed help teaching their 13-year-old son English. Without hesitation, Dominica embraced the opportunity, offering English lessons and even delivering traditional Ukrainian meals.

None of us really know where our respective journeys will lead. I doubt my mom, when she left war-torn Ukraine at the tender age of 5, ever imagined that 80 years later she would have borne witness from afar of all the turmoil that her homeland has endured over the past eight decades. Possibly the worst of which occurred in 2022 when Russia invaded the country. Nevertheless, she continues to hold her head high, praying for peace in Ukraine, and in the United States, and throughout the world. Her hopeful and resilient mindset remains unshaken.

Dominica with her sister Sonya, their husbands and parents.

Dominica's daughter Yvonne, Son in-law Joe, and their children Olivia, Victoria and Frankie.

Dominica's parents.

Dominica with her sister Sonya and their parents.

Dominica and her sister Sonya.

Dominica and her family 1970

Dominica with her husband Frank, and four daughters Michelle, Yvonne, Andrea,and Francine for their 60th wedding anniversary.

Dominica and Frank with their daughter Yvonne (husband Joe).

Dominica with her husband Frank, daughter Michelle, and her three children, Annese (husband Andy), Dominica and Joely.

Dominica's daughter Michelle (partner Paula) and Michelle's three daughters.

Family picture

Dominica's daughter Andrea (husband Dave) and her two children Nathaniel and Nicolette (husband Ryan).

Family Picture

Dominica and her daughter Michelle.

Dominica and Frank with one of their great-grandsons.

Dominica and Frank with one of their great-grandaughters.

Dominica with her daughter Yvonne, grandaughter and great grandaughter

Dominica's daughter Francine (husband Ray), and their three sons Luke, Matthew and John.

Dominica and Frank with one of their great-grandaughters.

About the Authors:

Kate Graney is a Professor of Political Science at Skidmore College, where she teaches classes in the history and politics of the former Soviet Union as well as in human rights, peace studies, and gender and international relations. She is the author of two books, including  *Russia, the Former Soviet Republics and Europe Since 1989: Transformation and Tragedy* (Oxford University Press, 1999). A native of western New York, she enjoys hiking, skiing, reading, and learning.

Kaitlin McQuade is a third-year student at Skidmore College. Her major is in Political Science and her minors are American Studies and International Affairs. She was born and raised in New York City but nowadays spends most of her year in Saratoga Springs. When she is not in class or studying, she enjoys taking her dog on walks, swimming laps, and watching movies with her family.

Francine Annese Apy -
Contributor

Francine, the youngest of Dominica's four daughters, holds a Bachelor of Arts from LeMoyne College and is pursuing her Masters in Applied Positive Psychology (MAPP) at the University of Pennyslyvania. With over 25 years of experience as an HR Executive and partner in a technology company, she has made her mark. In 2023, she embarked on a new journey by founding SoulFilling, LLC a company dedicated to being a beacon for the adoption community and beyond.

Francine is the author of a children's adoption themed book titled "Brianna's Brave Day at School." She illuminates the path of adoption with heartwarming stories of love, connection, and hope. Francine passionately embraces the diverse tapestry of adoption narratives, advocating for open and honest conversations about adoption within our homes, schools, work and communities.

In addition to her professional and advocacy work, Francine has been happily married for over three decades and is the proud mother of three grown sons, all blessings of adoption. For leisure, you'll find her traveling with family and friends and enjoying walks with her two loyal labs, Hudson, and Henry. A dedicated writer and avid reader, she is a strong person of faith, a yoga enthusiast, and always on a quest to meet new people and expand her knowledge and horizons.